DAYS THAT CHANGED THE WORLD

THE FIRST
TEST-TUBE BABY

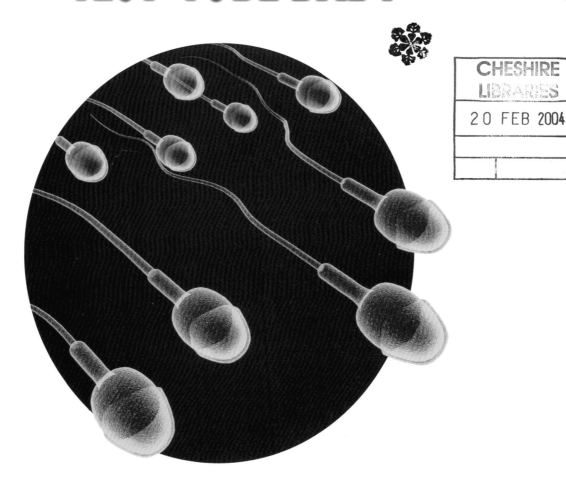

Fiona Macdonald

ticktock
MEDIA

Copyright © ticktock Entertainment Ltd 2003
First published in Great Britain in 2003 by ticktock Media Ltd.,
Unit 2, Orchard Business Centre, North Farm Road, Tunbridge Wells, Kent, TN2 3XF
ISBN 1 86007 420 0 pbk
ISBN 1 86007 427 8 hbk
Printed in Taiwan
A CIP catalogue record for this book is available from the British Library.

CONTENTS

INTRODUCTION *4–7*

BEFORE *fertility & infertility* *8–15*

FEELINGS OF CHANGE *understanding infertility* *16–21*

THE CRITICAL MOMENT *a new hope* *22–29*

AFTERMATH *mixed reactions* *30–33*

LATER *tried & tested* *34–39*

FUTURE *looking forward* *40–41*

TIMELINE *42–43*

GLOSSARY *44–45*

INDEX *46–47*

ACKNOWLEDGEMENTS *48*

This ancient South American fertility charm would have been carried by a woman hoping to increase her fertility.

Louise Brown, the world's first test-tube baby, celebrated her second birthday with a party.

On July 25th, 1978, at three minutes to midnight, a healthy baby girl was born at Oldham General Hospital in Lancashire, in the north of England. Her name was Louise Brown, and her birth made medical history. She was the first-ever baby, anywhere in the world, to be born as the result of an experimental new treatment designed to help infertile couples conceive a baby. The treatment's scientific name was 'IVF' (you can read more about this on p.22) but most people called Louise the 'test-tube baby'.

Before the development of this amazing technique, childless couples were forced to accept their infertility. Traditionally, it was believed to be the woman's fault – and these women would be labelled 'barren' and shunned by society. However, thanks to scientific developments in the 19th and 20th centuries, doctors began to gain a proper understanding of infertility. By the 1960s, scientists began to look at ways of tackling the complex problem of infertility.

In 1965, thanks to the work of two British doctors, Dr Robert Edwards and Dr Patrick Steptoe, a new treatment called IVF was made available for the first time to help childless couples.

When Mr and Mrs Brown were told of the new, experimental treatment for infertility, they were very excited and put themselves forward for the programme. Amazingly, less than one year later, Louise was born. Louise Brown's birth also marked the end of long years of painstaking research by a pioneering medical team, which had been working with infertile couples since 1966. But, until Mrs Brown gave birth to Louise, they had not been successful, despite a series of attempts.

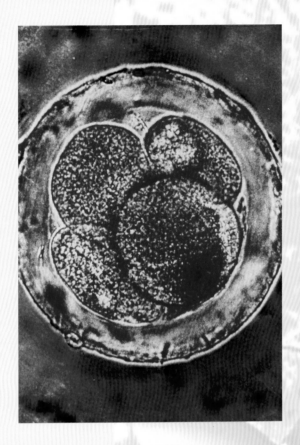

During IVF treatment, ripe eggs are taken from the woman and fertilized by a man's sperm in the laboratory, before being implanted back into the woman's body. After this point, the egg grows normally, as shown in this electron microscope photograph.

The discovery of IVF led to the birth of hundreds of thousands of babies, and also to a dramatic increase in the number of twins, triplets, quads, quintets and even septuplets!

INTRODUCTION

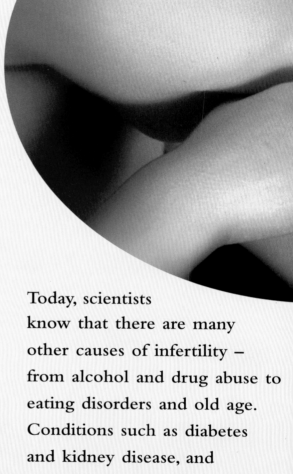

In 1978, when Louise Brown was born, the IVF technique used to treat her parents seemed shocking. But it was just one of many exciting scientific breakthroughs – along with organ transplants, gene therapy and cloning – that were taking place in the second half of the 20th century. These breakthroughs revolutionized our understanding of the body and how it works.

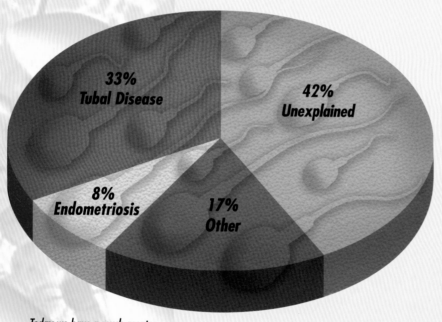

Today we have a much greater understanding of why some couples are unable to have children. Problems with the Fallopian tubes are the most common reason for infertility, but in over 40% of cases, doctors are still unable to pinpoint a reason for the problem.

33% Tubal Disease

42% Unexplained

8% Endometriosis

17% Other

Today, scientists know that there are many other causes of infertility – from alcohol and drug abuse to eating disorders and old age. Conditions such as diabetes and kidney disease, and environmental factors such as exposure to pollutants may also cause infertility. Scientific findings also led to new ways of controlling fertility, such as the contraceptive pill.

The IVF breakthrough led to new treatments for infertility and a greater understanding of what causes the problem.

The IVF technique that produced Louise Brown, and thousands more test-tube babies after her, brought great to their height and the colour of their eyes. Further possibilities, such as cloning, raise the spectre of creating babies in an entirely unnatural way. This idea became more real when the bizarre Raelian Movement announced in 2002 that they had created the world's first cloned baby, 'Eve'. Although this claim has not been proven, and reproductive cloning is illegal in most countries, it represents a glimpse into other possible results of IVF research.

happiness to her parents and gave hope to childless couples all around the world. IVF research also contributed to the discovery of new treatments for several serious diseases.

However, like many important scientific discoveries, IVF also raised important and difficult questions for individuals and societies to consider. These questions involved ethical dilemmas such as the possibility of creating 'designer babies' – where parents might be able to customize their children, down

After just 21 weeks, a human foetus is already recognisable. It will be able to hear and open its eyes, and can already recognise its mother's voice.

Rael (left), is the leader of the Raelian Movement – a cult who believe life was created in space. The movement also claim to have created the world's first cloned baby, 'Eve', with more cloned children to follow in the future.

Attitudes towards children vary from century to century and from culture to culture, but one thing has never changed anywhere: becoming a parent brings joy and fulfilment. This painting by the French Impressionist Renoir shows a happy family enjoying a day out.

Why do couples get married or set up home together? The reasons vary from time to time. Some are emotional: people fall in love, or hope to find companionship. Others are practical. In some countries, moving in with a partner is the only way of leaving the parental home. But almost everywhere, most couples agree that their family life is not complete without children. However, for some people making this step is not so easy, and they have problems producing their own children.

Fulfilment Becoming a parent creates a great sense of fulfilment, joy and responsibility. Many men and women feel that raising a happy, healthy family is the most important activity in their lives. In certain communities, being a parent earns you extra respect. This is why some people in Arabic-speaking societies change their names when their first son is born. They become known as 'Abu' (father of) or 'Umm' (mother of), followed by the new baby's name.

Security In countries where there are no state benefits to rely upon, children are valued for an additional reason. They are useful! They run errands, care for younger brothers and sisters, and sometimes go out to work. They are an 'insurance policy' – a way of providing comfort and security in old age. In most African and Asian cultures, children are expected to care for their aged parents.

LOVED *and valued*

Although today, some people choose not to have children, the vast majority decide to raise a family. Over 2,500 years ago, a Hebrew poet wrote: *'Happy is the man who has his quiver full of children.'* Around 150 BC, Roman noblewoman Cornelia praised her sons, saying, *'These children are my jewels.'*

Name and fame
For rich and powerful people, having a child is sometimes essential if they wish to pass on their land, wealth or titles to future generations. Rulers throughout history have hoped to produce sons who would reign after them – although few could match the example of Pharaoh Ramses II of ancient Egypt (who reigned from 1279 to 1213 BC). He fathered more than 100 children by many different wives.

Reproduction
In the 20th century, scientists suggested an additional reason for why so many men and women feel that they simply must, if possible, produce a child. The theory is that our genes – the chemical code inside cells that determines what we look like and how we grow – are 'selfish'. They want to live for ever, by passing themselves on from generation to generation. Before pregnancy can start, and a baby can be born, a woman has to conceive. Conception is a complex and delicate process. But it is also very common – countless billions of babies have been conceived since the first humans evolved. For these reasons, conception is often known as 'an everyday miracle'. But what is it, and how does it happen?

Conception
Conception is a three-stage process that takes between seven and ten days to complete. It involves the production of an egg and some sperm, the fertilization of the egg, and the implantation of the fertilized, fast-growing egg into the lining of the woman's uterus (womb).

'I have often wished for the blessing of motherhood… With it, and through the varied experiences that accompany it, I could perhaps have achieved something better than that which I have… until now.'

Part of a letter written in 1849 by Swedish opera star Jenny Lind, one of the most famous and successful women of her day. In spite of her brilliant achievements, she still believed that having a child would be a more worthwhile thing to do.

In some of the world's poorer countries, parents bring their children to the fields. When they are old enough, the children will take on a share of the work.

FERTILITY *facts*

- It takes about 45 minutes for sperm to reach the Fallopian tubes.
- A sperm can stay alive in the Fallopian tubes for about three days, ready to fuse with an egg.
- Sperm can be male or female. They determine whether the fertilized egg will grow into a girl or a boy.
- A woman's ovaries contain about 35,000 immature eggs. Only about 500 will ever mature and have the chance to be fertilized.

Many women feel happy and excited by pregnancy, but others find it a difficult time. They may feel sick, exhausted and 'not themselves' while pregnant.

Eggs and sperm

Most adult humans produce special cells designed for reproduction. In women these cells are called eggs, in men they are called sperm. They are made and stored in sex organs — two testes in men, two ovaries in women — that mature when a child reaches puberty (usually in early teenage years). Each egg or sperm contains only half the chromosomes (genetic information) needed to make up a normal body cell. To survive, they must fuse (join together), linking the two sets of chromosomes. If they do this, they create a new cell, containing enough genetic information to become a new life.

Fertilization

Eggs and sperm normally join together during sexual intercourse. Sperm produced by the man's testes swim along the woman's vagina, into the uterus, and then enter the Fallopian tubes. There, just one sperm fuses with an egg. It burrows through the egg's outer surface so that its chromosomes can combine with those belonging to the egg. This process is called fertilization.

Division

As soon as an egg is fertilized, it starts to grow. It divides into two cells, then each of those cells divides again. This process continues rapidly. After 72 hours, the fertilized egg's cells have divided 32 times, and it contains 64 cells in total. Once it has reached this stage, the egg begins to travel down the Fallopian tubes until it reaches the uterus. This journey can take up to seven days.

Implantation

While the egg travels, it grows tiny finger-like projections around its outer edge. These projections burrow into the uterus's lining, and help the cells of the fertilized egg draw nourishment from the lining's rich blood supply. This process is called 'nidation' or 'implantation'. Now, at last, conception is complete and a pregnancy has begun. A mother can look forward to having her baby.

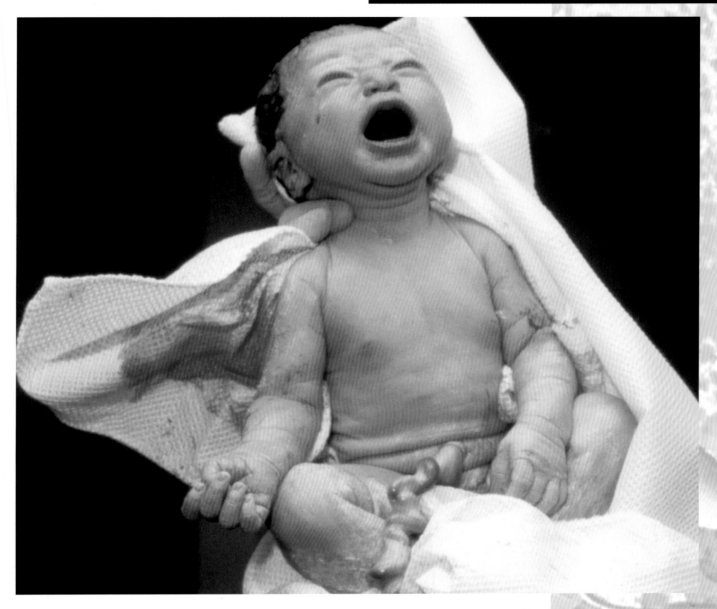

Infertility Unfortunately, not all people who want children are able to have them naturally. Doctors estimate that as many as one in six couples are infertile. These couples may have to wait for many years before the woman conceives, or she may fail to conceive at all. Today, we understand a great number of the scientific reasons for infertility. But in the past, people did not know why it happened and there were many superstitious beliefs surrounding fertility.

Parents never forget the experience of holding their baby for the first time, immediately after he or she has been born. The baby is still attached to its umbilical cord at this time. This will be cut and tied by doctors to produce a 'belly button'.

OVULATION

Men can produce sperm at almost any time, but a woman only produces an egg, on average, about 12 times a year. This is called 'ovulation'. Every month, about 14 days before her period, one of her ovaries releases a ripened egg. It travels into the nearest Fallopian tube, where it lives for about 12 hours. If it is not fertilized by a sperm, it dies.

Queen Anne Boleyn, Henry VIII's wife, was a victim of the prejudiced beliefs about pregnancy that were common in the 16th century and for a long time afterwards. We now know that her husband's blood type probably played a part in her failure to produce a second child.

GOD'S *gift*

People from many faiths have often seen fertility as a gift from God. For example, one 16th-century book, designed to teach people about the Roman Catholic faith, stated: *'Married people, having received the gracious gift of fertility from God, which He does not give to everybody, must give humbly Him thanks every time a child is born.'* Many religious leaders still hold similar views today. They oppose abortion and contraception, because they believe that only God has the power to decide whether a couple should have a child.

Supernatural Even today, the birth of a new baby is often seen as a miraculous event. So it is not surprising that, in the past, people looked for magical reasons to explain why couples could not have children. They blamed infertility on bad luck, witchcraft, or as a punishment sent by God for sins that the couple had committed.

Charms and rituals To protect themselves from any evil influences that might prevent them from becoming pregnant, mothers wore magic amulets, or carried lucky charms. They took part in complicated rituals, designed to increase their fertility. Often these involved symbols of new life, such as eggs. They said prayers, gave offerings and made pilgrimages to holy places, to ask their god or gods to send them the gift of a child.

The woman's fault?
Today we know that both men and women can be infertile, but in the past infertility was almost always believed to be the woman's fault. It was very shameful for a woman to be labelled 'barren'. It meant that she had failed in her most important duty — to have children.

Punishing 'failure'
In many countries, a husband could divorce a wife if she failed to give birth. King Henry VIII, who ruled England from 1509 to 1547, is famous for marrying six times in the hope of producing a male heir to succeed him to the throne. His second wife, Anne Boleyn, produced a daughter but then gave birth to a stillborn (dead) son — probably because her blood was of a type called rhesus negative (see box). Because of this, she was accused of witchcraft, put on trial, found guilty and beheaded! In the past, couples who

could not give birth to their own children found other ways of having a family. They adopted children (became their legal parents) or fostered them (agreed to care for them for a period of time). Children put into the care of childless couples might be foundlings (children who had been abandoned at special hospitals), children born to sick, unwed, or overworked mothers, or orphans whose parents had died.

THE RHESUS *factor*

Human blood contains many different chemicals, including certain types known together as 'rhesus factor'. Some people's blood does not have this; they are therefore 'rhesus negative'. If an egg from a rhesus negative woman is fertilized by sperm from a man who has rhesus factor, her unborn child's blood will probably contain rhesus factor too, and her immune system will be sensitive to it. This will not affect her first child, but if she conceives a second baby with rhesus factor, her immune system will create antibodies (killer cells) to fight against it. These can seriously damage the unborn baby, and any future babies with similar blood.

This ancient South American fertility charm would have been carried by a woman hoping to increase her fertility.

Most adoptive or foster parents have a very rewarding relationship with their children, who grow up in a loving family environment.

Given away Until about 1900, childless couples living in Europe or the USA might ask a relative to give them a child to bring up as their own, especially if the relative had several children of their own. In many cultures, such as those found in West Africa and the Caribbean, it was also common for parents to send some of their children to be fostered with relatives, who cared for them, brought them up and provided them with schooling or taught them useful skills.

No choice Often, these children were greatly loved, and given many advantages. But they were very rarely consulted, or asked to consent to a move that would dramatically change their lives. Being adopted or fostered meant that these children lost close contact with their entire family, including parents, brothers and sisters for a long while – and sometimes for ever.

THE BEST *thing*

In most countries, becoming an adoptive parent is a long process. Couples undergo detailed psychological examinations, and social workers investigate their private lives. But many feel that these procedures are all worthwhile, for the sake of adopting a longed-for child.

Happy together Unfortunately, there were sometimes cruel and abusive adoptive or foster parents and unhappy, badly treated children – just as there are in all other families. However, on the whole, adoption and fostering arrangements have provided millions of infertile couples and their adopted and fostered children with happy and full family lives.

New ideas In the late 20th century, ideas about adoption changed. Experts believed it was better for children to stay with their natural parents where possible, and offered help and support to families facing problems. Improved methods of birth control – especially the contraceptive pill – meant that fewer 'unwanted' babies were born. Changing social attitudes meant that it became perfectly acceptable for an unmarried woman – or man – to bring up a child by themselves. At the same time, well-meaning childless couples from wealthy countries who adopted babies born in poor or war-torn nations were criticized for taking children away from their homeland and their heritage.

'Something must be done' Many childless couples were becoming less willing to accept infertility as 'bad luck', or 'God's punishment'. These couples spoke out to doctors and scientists that 'something should be done' to resolve their childless state. And as childbirth in wealthy countries became safer and less painful – thanks to advances in medical techniques – fewer women than before were prepared to be childless if it could be avoided. Unlike women in the past or women in poor countries today, terrible suffering or death were known to be unlikely outcomes of childbirth for most 20th-century women.

With the changing attitudes of the 1960s, people felt less influenced by the Church's teachings on marriage, pregnancy and fertility. In particular, society's attitudes began changing towards unmarried mothers, and new social-security benefits improved their situation.

'Your pink, healthy face will turn sickly green... your eyes will lose their sparkle. Your belly will swell and you will have indigestion and pains in your side. Your back will ache. You will look pale and ill ... no longer beautiful ... and everything you eat will make you feel sick. You will be unable to sleep at night, because you will worry so much about the pain of giving birth.'

Advice to young women by a 13th-century European priest, encouraging them to stay virgins and avoid pregnancy.

In the past, doctors wanting to treat infertility faced a major problem. The female reproductive system was hidden deep inside the body, and was very difficult to observe. For centuries, no-one really understood how women's bodies were made, and religious leaders in many countries forbade dissection (the cutting up of dead people) to investigate. Then, around 1500, doctors inspired by Renaissance ideas that encouraged exploration and scientific inquiry began to examine real bodies, and published their findings for others to study.

Andreas Vesalius (1514–64) founded the modern science of anatomy. His beautifully illustrated books were the first to show details of the human body in an accurate way.

1537–1543 Flemish doctor Andreas Vesalius, a professor at the university of Padua, Italy, published *Six Anatomical Pictures* and *On How the Human Body is Made*. Unlike earlier doctors, who had to draw their knowledge about the insides of the human body from studying animals and the writings of ancient wise men, Vesalius made his discoveries by dissecting humans. His books marked the start of a whole new approach to the study of anatomy and disease.

1561 Italian anatomist Gabriele Falloppia, who followed Vesalius as a professor at Padua, published *Anatomical Observations*. In this, he described in detail the tubes that carry eggs from

CUTTING UP *criminals*

Vesalius cut up the corpses of executed criminals to make his investigations. On one occasion, he even robbed a wayside gibbet and carried away the skeleton hanging there so that he could look at it more closely.

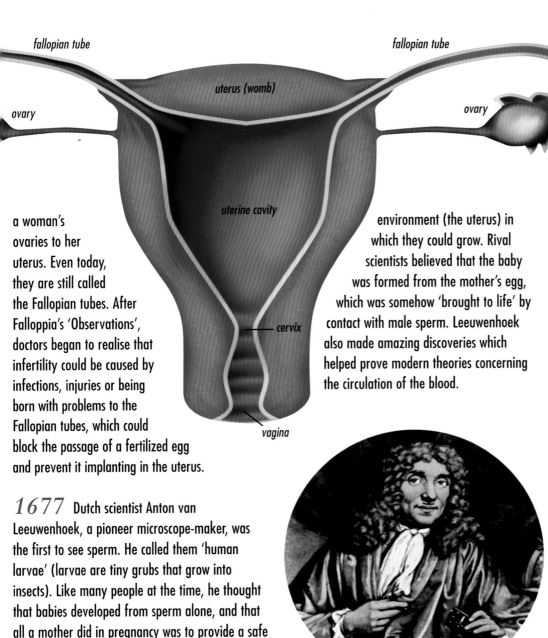

fallopian tube

fallopian tube

uterus (womb)

ovary

ovary

uterine cavity

cervix

vagina

A woman's ovaries produce one egg a month, that travels down the Fallopian tubes to the uterus. If this egg comes into contact with a man's sperm, the fertilized egg implants into the uterine lining and begins to develop into a baby. When the baby is ready to be born, the strong uterus muscles push it out during labour.

a woman's ovaries to her uterus. Even today, they are still called the Fallopian tubes. After Falloppia's 'Observations', doctors began to realise that infertility could be caused by infections, injuries or being born with problems to the Fallopian tubes, which could block the passage of a fertilized egg and prevent it implanting in the uterus.

1677 Dutch scientist Anton van Leeuwenhoek, a pioneer microscope-maker, was the first to see sperm. He called them 'human larvae' (larvae are tiny grubs that grow into insects). Like many people at the time, he thought that babies developed from sperm alone, and that all a mother did in pregnancy was to provide a safe

environment (the uterus) in which they could grow. Rival scientists believed that the baby was formed from the mother's egg, which was somehow 'brought to life' by contact with male sperm. Leeuwenhoek also made amazing discoveries which helped prove modern theories concerning the circulation of the blood.

As well as researching fertility, Leeuwenhoek also made important discoveries about bacteria.

It is a truth too well known, that mothers and their children are daily, if not hourly, destroyed (such is the practice of midwifery in our days) by ignorant wretches … a pack of young boys and old superannuated [retired] washerwomen, who are so impudent and inhuman as to … practise, even in the most difficult cases.

Comment by an 'expert' male midwife, keen to encourage new techniques, London, 1785

SPERM *matters*

On average, a man produces about 20 billion sperm every month, and around 400 million enter a woman's body each time a couple makes love. Each sperm is tiny – far too small to see with the naked eye. Sperm were first seen, under early microscopes, in the 17th century. But it was only in the 19th century that scientists finally understood the role sperm play in conception.

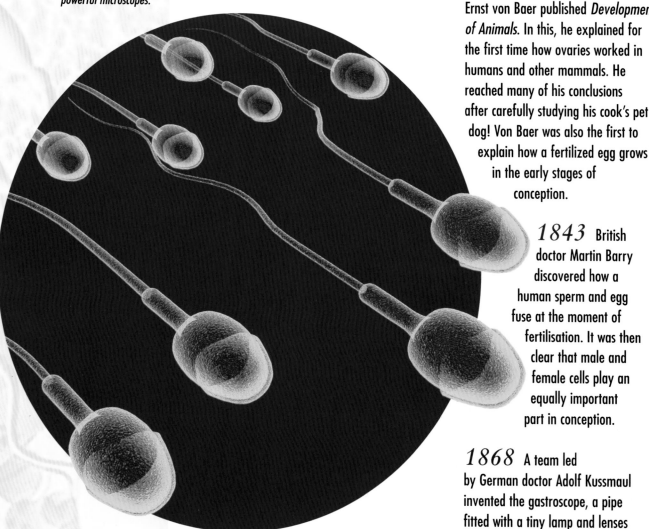

These tiny sperm are revealed in incredible detail by a scanning electron microscope (SEM), one of today's most powerful microscopes.

1700–1800 New discoveries about female anatomy improved midwifery techniques. This made childbirth less dangerous for many women. It also helped to prevent infertility resulting from injuries to a woman while her baby was being born. But it took a long time for the latest scientific discoveries to reach traditional female midwives and inexperienced male doctors.

1828–1837 Estonian scientist Karl Ernst von Baer published *Developmental History of Animals*. In this, he explained for the first time how ovaries worked in humans and other mammals. He reached many of his conclusions after carefully studying his cook's pet dog! Von Baer was also the first to explain how a fertilized egg grows in the early stages of conception.

1843 British doctor Martin Barry discovered how a human sperm and egg fuse at the moment of fertilisation. It was then clear that male and female cells play an equally important part in conception.

1868 A team led by German doctor Adolf Kussmaul invented the gastroscope, a pipe fitted with a tiny lamp and lenses that allowed him to see inside the human stomach — with the help of a fairground sword-swallower! Other doctors used this invention to develop the laparoscope, a tube inserted through a tiny cut in the abdomen. The laparoscope allowed them to examine reproductive organs in great detail. Today, fibre-optic endoscopes are made of bundles of glass fibres that transmit light. They are flexible, and can 'see' all around the organs, and even inside them.

LESS FERTILE *in old age*

For thousands of years, people have recognized that young men are more fertile than older ones. Around 1000 BC, an Egyptian scribe recorded this traditional medical advice. *'Marry a wife while you are young, so that she may give you many children.'* At that time, people did not know why older men are often less fertile than younger ones. Today, doctors think that sperm are weaker, and more likely to have defects, once a man is past 50 years old.

1929–1930 American scientists Edgar Allen, a zoologist; and Edward Doisy, a biologist, identified the main female sex hormone, called 'oestrogen'. This causes women to become sexually mature and thickens the lining of the uterus so it is ready for a fertilized egg. Allen had experimented by injecting laboratory mice with fluid from pigs' ovaries.

1934 German biochemist Adolf Butenandt discovered the second main female sex hormone, 'progesterone'. This hormone prepares the Fallopian tubes and the uterus to receive a fertilized egg, and helps a pregnancy to become firmly established. Butenandt received the Nobel Prize for Science in 1939 for his work.

The American doctor Edward Doisy received the Nobel Prize for Medicine for his work in the field of infertility in 1943.

> 'As recently as twelve years ago, very little was known about the nature of the sex hormones. Butenandt has made the first big step forward.'

The 1939 Nobel Prize awards panel give their speech when presenting Adolf Butenandt with his prize.

A SIMPLE *solution*

Some men have solved their infertility problems by changing their underpants! Tight-fitting clothes hold the testes (where sperm is produced) very close to the body. This increases their temperature, and can damage sperm. Wearing looser, baggier underwear keeps the testes cooler and can allow healthier sperm to develop.

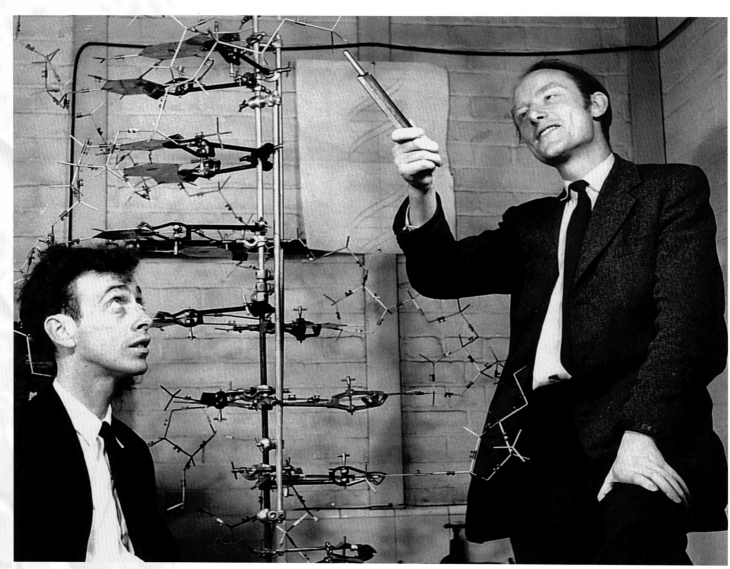

Francis Crick and James Watson were together awarded the Nobel prize for their discovery of DNA in 1953. They are pictured here with their famous molecular model of the DNA double helix.

1953 British biologist Francis Crick and American biologist James Watson discovered the double-helix structure of DNA (deoxyribonucleic acid) — the genetic material contained within the cells of all living things. Until this discovery, scientists were not precisely sure what happened when a sperm fertilized an egg. DNA showed how, in fertilization, genetic information from both parents combined to create a new and completely unique individual.

1957 Scottish doctor Ian Donald pioneered the use of ultrasound to monitor the development of an unborn baby inside a woman's uterus. His machines used soundwaves, too high for human ears to hear, to create pictures of the organs inside the body. These pictures helped doctors to see whether a pregnancy was progressing normally, and to examine a woman's uterus, ovaries and Fallopian tubes for any possible causes of infertility.

IN THE *wrong place*

An ectopic pregnancy is one where the fertilized egg implants and starts to grow outside the mother's uterus. It can happen naturally, as well as after fertility treatment. Ectopic pregancies are very dangerous, because the growing baby can cause serious internal bleeding that can kill the mother. They are terminated to avoid endangering the mother.

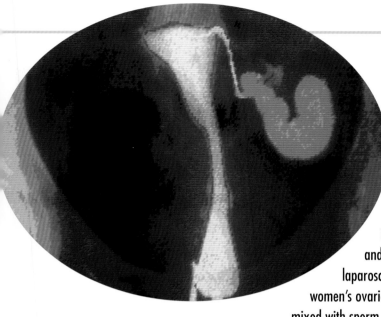

A colour x-ray showing damaged Fallopian tubes. Here, the tube on the right (blue) is blocked near the uterus (light blue triangle).

1965 British biologist Dr Robert Edwards developed new techniques for treating women with damaged Fallopian tubes. The techniques had previously only been used on animals. Edwards' plan was to mix sperm with unripe eggs taken from ovaries. He had developed a culture medium (mixture of chemicals) in which living cells, like eggs, could grow. However, Edwards found it very difficult to keep the unripe eggs alive and the technique was not a success.

1966 Dr Edwards teamed up with British gynaecologist (a doctor specialising in women's reproductive health) Dr Patrick Steptoe to work on new treatments for childless couples. Dr Steptoe had experience of using laparoscopes to investigate infertility. Together, Steptoe and Edwards decided to use a laparoscope to collect ripe eggs from women's ovaries. These eggs would then be mixed with sperm in the laboratory in the hope of fertilizing them. To make sure their patients produced a good supply of eggs, Edwards and Steptoe gave women powerful hormones to stimulate the ovaries.

1972 Edwards and Steptoe placed the eggs they had fertilized in their laboratory back inside the bodies of women with damaged Fallopian tubes. They hoped the fertile eggs would implant in the uterus, and develop into babies in the normal way. In 1975, a British woman called Marlene Platt became pregnant using this method, but very sadly, her pregnancy was ectopic (see box) and had to be terminated.

> ''*I have recovered at least all my former vigour ... My digestion and the working of my bowels have also improved considerably ... I find mental work easier than for years....*''
>
> *French experimenter Charles Brown-Séquard, an early pioneer in the study of hormones, made the following claim after he had injected himself with extracts from the testes of guinea-pigs and dogs in 1889.*

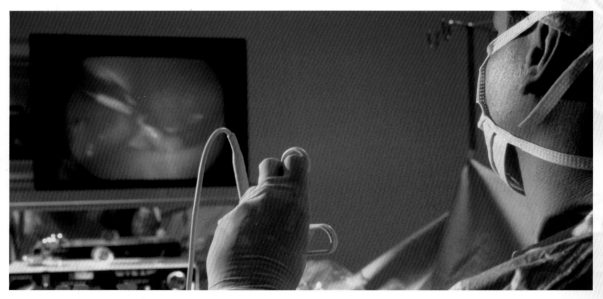

Robert Edwards and Patrick Steptoe had been close to making a major scientific breakthrough for years, but would they succeed in achieving their goal — the world's first artificially-inseminated birth?

THE CRITICAL MOMENT *a new hope*

John Brown, the father of the first test-tube baby, Louise Joy Brown.

Lesley and John Brown were an ordinary couple. They lived in Bristol, a city in the west of England, where Mr Brown was a railway worker. They did not set out to break records, become famous, take part in experiments, or be pioneers. However, in 1976 they made an extraordinary risky decision that made medical history and gave hope to millions of would-be parents all around the world.

NEW SCIENCE 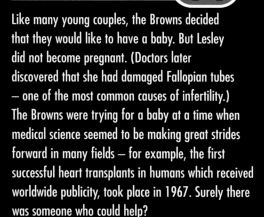 1975

Like many young couples, the Browns decided that they would like to have a baby. But Lesley did not become pregnant. (Doctors later discovered that she had damaged Fallopian tubes — one of the most common causes of infertility.) The Browns were trying for a baby at a time when medical science seemed to be making great strides forward in many fields — for example, the first successful heart transplants in humans which received worldwide publicity, took place in 1967. Surely there was someone who could help?

VISIT TO OLDHAM 1976

A doctor who had heard of the pioneering work by Dr Edwards and Dr Steptoe suggested that the Browns consult them. News of their experimental 'IVF' treatment (see box) was just becoming known. Dr Steptoe was working at Oldham General Hospital, in the north of England. He had all the equipment there to carry out IVF treatment, such as a special incubator to keep eggs at the right temperature after they are removed from the woman's body. The junior doctors, nurses and midwives at Oldham were also experienced in caring for women trying to become pregnant using the new technique. Hopeful that this might be their chance to have a baby at last, the Browns visited Oldham to see Dr Steptoe.

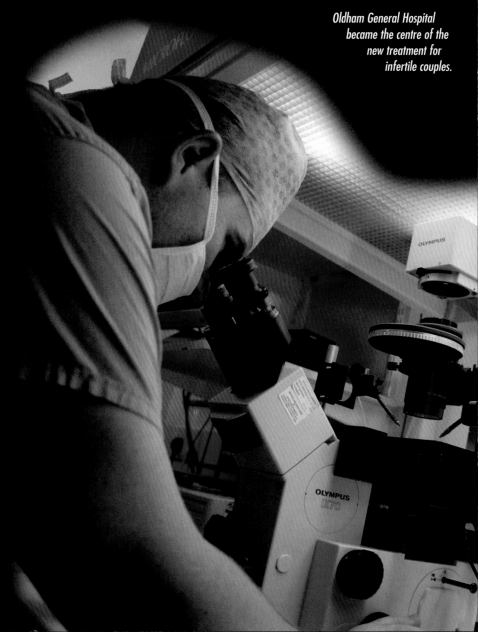

Oldham General Hospital became the centre of the new treatment for infertile couples.

VIEWS *from the ground*

'It was a very hard time as human nature makes you look for someone to blame and I didn't have anyone, it was my body. It was even harder to cope with the fact that I was responsible for putting my husband through this daily torture.'

A woman suffering emotional distress from infertility.

'For around five weeks prior to our first attempt I was having daily injections. I found it mentally quite difficult to put a needle into myself, but I only had to think, "Well, if you don't, you won't have a baby", and I managed.'

A woman who had IVF treatment.

'There is quite a lot of anxiety till you find out from the lab how many embryos have fertilized.... sometimes, even though the eggs and sperm look excellent, there may be a total failure of fertilization.'

A doctor specializing in infertility treatment.

THE RIGHT PATIENTS?

1977

Before IVF treatment could start, Dr Steptoe had to make sure that the Browns were suitable patients — physically and emotionally. Were they young and fit? Did they produce healthy eggs and sperm? Could they cope with the stress of lengthy medical treatment, with painful injections and blood tests, intimate examinations, powerful drugs and constant monitoring by nurses and doctors? He also had to warn them that there was no guarantee that his treatment would succeed. After almost 80 attempts, and one tragic termination, the treatment had not produced a baby so far. Could they face the prospect of failure?

The Browns were given powerful drugs during treatment to help boost their chances of making a baby.

Lesley and John Brown agreed to go ahead with the IVF treatment that was offered to them. Even today, more than 20 years after the first IVF treatments, infertile couples still do not find this an easy decision to make. Then, it was a brave step into the unknown.

Blood samples were taken regularly to determine whether the Browns were suitable for IVF.

THE PLAN

Dr Edwards and Dr Steptoe had made detailed plans for treating Mrs Brown. After so many earlier failures, they decided to change the procedure. Instead of giving Mrs Brown hormones to stimulate her ovaries into producing several ripened eggs, they decided to monitor her menstrual cycle, and 'harvest' just one ripe egg when it was naturally ready to be released from the ovary and travel down the Fallopian tube.

Nurses regularly took Mrs Brown's temperature to find the perfect time to take an egg from her.

EGG COLLECTING

The doctors calculated when one of Mrs Brown's eggs would be ready. She was then given an anaesthetic so that she would not feel pain, and a small cut was made in her abdomen. Gently, Dr Steptoe pushed a laparoscope through this opening, and examined Mrs Brown's ovaries. As everyone had hoped, there was a ripe egg, ready to collect. Using the laparoscope, he removed it and passed it over to Dr Edwards, who was waiting close by. Dr Edwards placed the egg in a glass dish and mixed it with some of Mr Brown's sperm, so that fertilization could take place. Then he added a special culture medium (liquid). This helped the egg and sperm to stay alive. Finally, he placed the dish in an incubator to keep it at the same temperature as the human body (37°C).

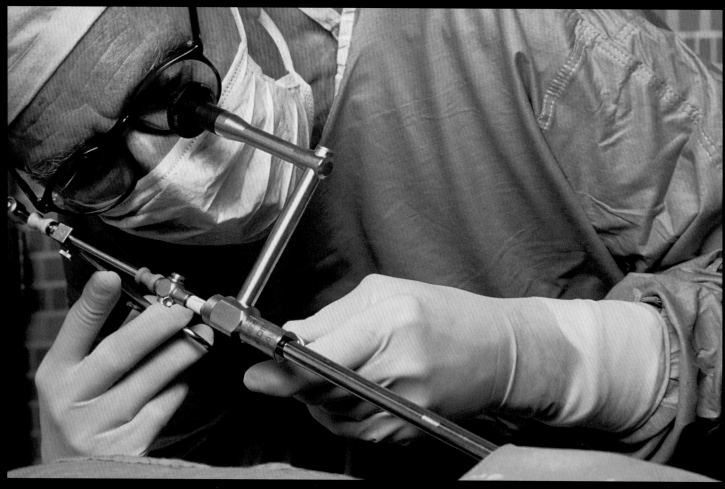

Doctors at Oldham General Hospital used a laparoscope to collect a ripe egg from Mrs Brown.

VIEWS *from the ground*

> "Motherhood is a gift. Plain and simple. We don't deserve it; we are graced with it, sometimes after much heartache."
>
> A woman suffering emotional distress from infertility.

> 'Counseling is not just needed during IVF treatment, but afterwards. I knew that if it didn't work this time, I would need help to accept it and to move on or try again.'
>
> A woman who had IVF treatment.

> 'The danger of IVF is that if you don't get pregnant after the treatment, you are likely to be very disappointed and disheartened.'
>
> A doctor specializing in IVF.

FERTILIZATION

11:11:77

Dr Edwards checked the dish to see whether the sperm had fertilized the eggs. They had! A new embryo was growing there and the cells of the egg had started to divide. The genetic material of the sperm was combining with the genetic material of the egg. Despite this, the team knew it was far too soon to celebrate. The most delicate and the most risky part of the procedure was yet to come.

The fertilized egg started to divide, just as doctors had hoped.

Doctors inserted the fertilized egg back into Mrs Brown.

RETURNING THE EGG

13:11:77

In earlier treatments, Dr Steptoe had waited four or five days before placing the embryo back inside a woman's body. This time, after discussions with Dr Edwards, he decided to put Mrs Brown's embryo back inside her body after only two-and-a-half days. A thin, flexible plastic tube carried the embryo through her vagina into the uterus.
After this, if all went well, the embryo would implant itself into the uterus lining — and Mrs Brown would have conceived!

VIEWS *from the ground*

'This period [14 days after the embryo is placed in the uterus] is often the hardest part of an IVF cycle for the patient, because of the suspense of waiting to find out if a pregnancy has occurred ... For many patients, these 14 days are often the longest days of their life!'

A doctor at Oldham General.

'Although my pregnancy went smoothly, it was emotionally draining ... I would have loved to have contact with ... someone who could just say that all my fears were normal, they felt the same....'

A woman who received IVF treatment.

'Every time you start [an IVF] cycle, you have to hope for the best and be prepared for the worst. Interestingly, we often find that couples going through a second IVF are much more relaxed and in control ... they are aware of all the medical minutiae and are better prepared for these.'

A doctor at Oldham General.

STAGES OF PREGNANCY

If a woman conceives and becomes pregnant, levels of a hormone called HCG rise in her body. In IVF treatments, these can be measured by taking a sample of blood, about 10–14 days after an embryo has been placed in her uterus. Mrs Brown's hormone levels were carefully monitored, and, by early December 1977, it became clear that she had conceived. This was an exciting – but anxious – time for the Browns and the whole medical team. Would this IVF treatment work, when so many others had failed? For the next eight months, Mrs Brown's progress was checked and observed, using many different techniques, such as ultrasound and amniocentesis. Everyone hoped that her pregnancy would follow a normal pattern.

Embryo at five weeks old.

1–10 WEEKS

The embryo grows very fast at this time. Its appearance changes from something like a tadpole to recognizable human form, and its size increases from about the size of a grain of rice at week four, to about 6 cm (2.5 in) at week ten. All its main organs – such as brain and lungs – develop, its heart begins to beat and its blood begins to flow. It has minute sex organs and tiny arms and legs – complete with fingers, toes and even fingerprints!

11–20 WEEKS

The embryo's skeleton changes from soft, stretchy cartilage to bone. After this stage, doctors call it a 'fetus'. Its digestive system develops, and tiny tooth-buds form inside its gums. By 16 weeks, its eyes can tell light from dark, and its ears can hear loud noises. It grows eyelashes, eyebrows and fingernails. By 20 weeks, it is about 25 cm (10 in) long and weighs about 350 g (12 oz). It can move, touch, feel and kick.

21-30 WEEKS

The fetus's brain grows and becomes more active. After about 23–24 weeks, it can probably feel pain. By 28 weeks, its eyes are open, it has excellent hearing, and can recognize its mother's voice. Its skin thickens and it looks plumper because it builds up stores of fat that will help regulate its temperature after it is born. It has regular times of sleeping and waking, and probably dreams. By 30 weeks, it is 40 cm (16 in) long and weighs about 1.5 kg (3 lbs).

Embryo at 21 weeks old.

31-40 WEEKS

Embryo at 32 weeks old.

The fetus puts on a lot more weight now — about 225 g (8 oz) each week. Its lungs grow and prepare to breathe oxygen. Its eyes are able to focus, its hands can grip, and its feet can make stepping movements. It responds to music, and can turn its head to look around. By 40 weeks, it is ready to be born.

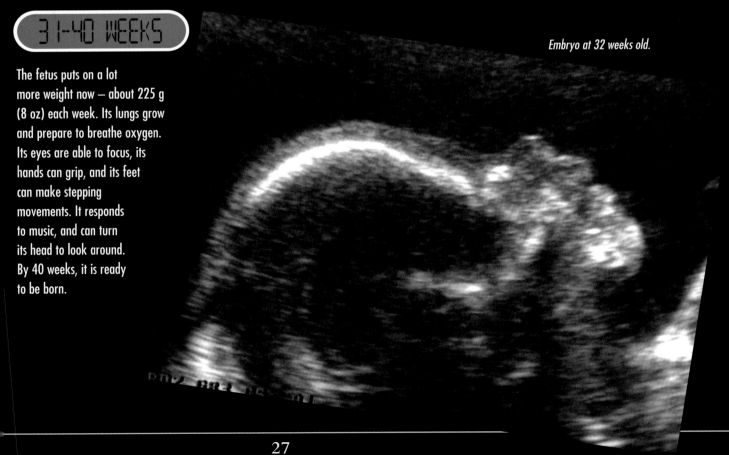

Dr Edwards and Dr Steptoe at a press conference to give the latest news on Mrs Brown.

PUBLIC UNEASE

Week by week, Mrs Brown's pregnancy progressed. She stayed healthy, and tests showed that the fetus was developing normally inside her uterus. However, when Dr Edwards and Dr Steptoe announced to the media that their treatment had achieved a pregnancy that was going well, the news was greeted with shock, surprise and alarm. Many people were intrigued and impressed, but just as many were doubtful. Some worried that being outside the uterus for a few days might have harmed the egg or the fertilized embryo, and that the baby might have serious disabilities. Others warned of the dangers of 'meddling with nature' or 'trying to play God', and prophesied that a monster might be born.

DANGEROUS PROBLEM  25:7:78

Dr Steptoe had calculated that Mrs Brown's baby was due to be born on August 3rd, 1978 – the end of the pregnancy was in sight. Everyone felt relieved that things had gone so well. They had hardly dared hope for this when the IVF treatment began. But suddenly, there were problems. Routine tests revealed that Mrs Brown was suffering from toxaemia. This is a condition (known as pre-eclampsia today) that can raise blood pressure to very high levels. Dr Steptoe knew that, if it was left untreated, it could lead to a much more serious condition, and that Mrs Brown and her unborn baby might both die.

OPERATION  22:00

Dr Steptoe decided that it would not be safe to let Mrs Brown's pregnancy continue. He would perform an operation – called a 'Caesarian section' – to deliver the baby and reduce the risk of any further problems developing. Late in the evening, Mrs Brown was taken to the operating theatre, along with a camera crew. In a Caesarian operation, the mother is given an anaesthetic so that she does not feel pain, and the doctor carefully cuts open her abdomen and then the uterus inside. An assistant removes the baby from the uterus and makes sure it is breathing while the doctor stitches up the cuts so that they will heal quickly and neatly.

A baby is being born by caesarian section.

VIEWS *from the ground*

'I am so happy I could cry. It was just like a dream.'
Mr Brown.

'She is a beautiful baby. She's got a very small amount of hair ....'
Camera operator who filmed the birth.

'Within five seconds of birth she let out the biggest yell you've heard a baby make'.
Dr Edwards.

'I've never seen a man so excited.'
Hospital worker, about Mr Brown.

'Mrs Brown You've Got a Lovely Daughter'
Words of popular song, widely quoted at the time.

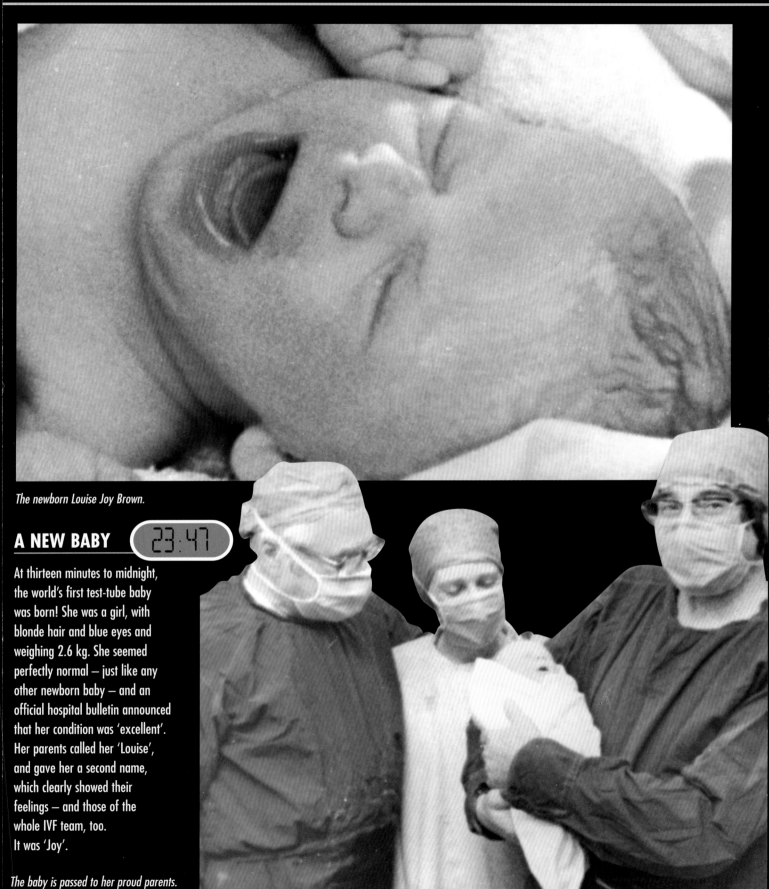

The newborn Louise Joy Brown.

A NEW BABY `23:47`

At thirteen minutes to midnight, the world's first test-tube baby was born! She was a girl, with blonde hair and blue eyes and weighing 2.6 kg. She seemed perfectly normal – just like any other newborn baby – and an official hospital bulletin announced that her condition was 'excellent'. Her parents called her 'Louise', and gave her a second name, which clearly showed their feelings – and those of the whole IVF team, too. It was 'Joy'.

The baby is passed to her proud parents.

Few people who heard the news could fail to share Mr and Mrs Brown's delight in producing a longed-for child. Many politicians, scientists and media commentators also hurried to congratulate Dr Steptoe and Dr Edwards for pioneering a 'world first' for British expertise.

> In 1978, the birth of Louise Brown was announced in dramatic newspaper headlines all over the world. Associated Press declared that she was a
>
> '...miracle child...'
>
> The magazine Good Housekeeping described the news as
>
> '...the most extraordinary birth in human history...'

Comfort and joy Louise was described as a 'miracle baby'. Her birth brought new hope to millions of couples all around the world as doctors learned from, and copied, Dr Edward's and Dr Steptoe's techniques. For many people, even the chance of IVF treatment brought tremendous comfort. As one doctor explained, 'The agony of childlessness is impossible to describe, and the joy after an infertile couple produces a child is also impossible to describe.' If further proof of this statement was needed, John and Lesley Brown agreed to undergo IVF treatment for a second time to complete their family – and produced a sister for Louise, whom they called Natalie.

Motherhood The ability to have children is particularly important in certain traditional societies, such as India. As Dr Brij Kalyan, of the Hope Infertility Clinic in Bangalore, commented in 1994, 'IVF is the best thing that could happen to the Indian woman, who is under tremendous pressure from many quarters to conceive and produce a child to prove her womanhood'. But not all women agreed. Some feminists argued that infertility should be seen as a social, not a medical, problem. Women should be valued for themselves, not just as mothers of the next generation.

Mr and Mrs Brown proudly showed Louise to the world's media. The sight of such a healthy, normal baby reassured many of those worried that the revolutionary technique might produce a 'monster'.

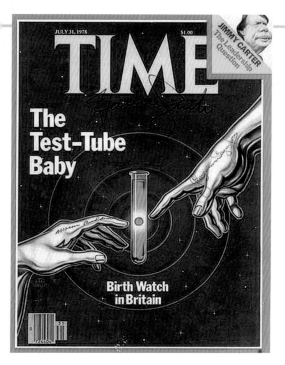

New uses

Some of the new uses for IVF techniques were fairly straightforward, such as breeding pedigree pigs or racehorses. They were welcomed by farmers and stock-breeders, who realised that it might be possible from now on to mate prize-winning animals from different countries without the difficulties and dangers of transporting valuable livestock by air or sea.

A frightening future?

Other uses were more controversial. They involved experiments with genetic engineering in which, for example, scientists tried to create plants that would not be damaged by frost or insect pests. In the future, scientists might also try screening embryos for 'defects' such as inherited diseases, before placing them back inside a women's bodies. Many people feared that this might make it too easy to create 'designer babies', chosen at embryo stage based on their potential strength, intelligence or good looks.

In an interview with Minnesota Public Radio in 1998, leading American gynaecologist Howard Jones declared:
'... with one procedure, suddenly it became possible to overcome a great many difficulties which seemed almost completely insurmountable prior to that.'

Together with his wife, Georgeanna (also a gynaecologist), Howard Jones performed the USA's first successful IVF procedure in 1981. In the 1960s, their research findings had helped Dr Edwards with some of his early fertility experiments.

Breakthrough

As news of Louise's birth spread around the globe, it was hailed as a great breakthrough, especially by other doctors who had been working to help infertile couples. They also recognized that the techniques developed by Edwards and Steptoe for keeping eggs, sperm and embryos alive and healthy outside the human body might be useful for many other purposes.

America's first test-tube baby, Elizabeth Jordan Carr, is seen here reading with her mother. She was born in Norfolk, Virginia, USA, in December 1981.

PLAYING *God*

Some people were worried about where IVF treatment might lead — even radical thinkers such as British Labour politician Leo Abse. He was well-known for supporting campaigns to reform UK laws relating to children, divorce, family planning and homosexuality. But in 1978, when Louise Brown was born, he commented: *'The issue is how far we play God, how far are we going to treat mankind as we would animal husbandry [breeding]'*.

Many films have been made of Mary Shelley's classic novel, Frankenstein. Much more than a horror story, the novel explores the implications of science interfering with nature.

In 1932, British novelist Aldous Huxley published a novel called *Brave New World*. In it, he imagined a country where babies were mass-produced in factories, like cars. They were conceived in test-tubes, and grown in large glass jars until they were ready to be born. All births were organized by the state, and babies were genetically engineered to be useful and obedient.

CARL LAEMMLE *presents*

FRANKENSTEIN

THE MAN WHO MADE A MONSTER

COLIN CLIVE, MAE CLARKE
JOHN BOLES, BORIS KARLOFF,
DWIGHT FRYE, EDWARD VAN SLOAN & FREDERIC KERR.
Based upon the
Mary Wollstonecroft Shelley Story
Adapted by JOHN L.BALDERSTON
from the play by PEGGY WEBLING

DIRECTED BY ... JAMES WHALE
PRODUCED BY.. CARL LAEMMLE, JR.
A UNIVERSAL PICTURE

Natural pregnancy and human feelings such as parental love — were banned. Huxley wrote his book as a way of criticizing his own times. But in 1978, after Louise Brown's birth was announced, some people feared that his nightmare vision might be coming true.

Birth of a monster? Some people compared Louise's birth to Mary Shelley's story, *Frankenstein*. Published in 1818, the book is about a medical student who puts together body parts in his laboratory and creates an uncontrollable monster. Some people believed that Louise was also a monster — even though medical tests suggested she was 'normal' in every way. They worried that she might not develop properly, that she would fall sick with an incurable genetic disease, or that she would grow old before her time.

A zombie with psychic powers? A few believed that Louise Brown's mind had been altered by IVF procedures, and that she had psychic powers. They claimed she could move objects just by looking at them! One group argued that because Louise had not been conceived in the way that God had intended, she was an 'empty shell' — like a zombie without a soul.

Breaking laws Many critics of IVF argued that the treatment broke human and holy laws, and that everyone involved might be punished (by future events, or by nature) as a result. For example, the Roman

Catholic church taught that unnatural ways of conceiving children was wrong, and warned that 'science without conscience can only lead to man's ruin'. Psychologists argued that IVF babies might feel that there was something bizarre, abnormal or shameful about the way in which

INTO THE *unknown*

Many scientists admired the techniques of Edwards and Steptoe. But they were still cautious about welcoming the test-tube baby technique. They realized that IVF could have unpredictable results. In 1978, one genetics expert summed up their views: *'When man is fumbling at the source of life, not even a brilliant physician as Dr Steptoe can read the consequences in advance.'*

they were conceived, and that this might ruin their lives. In the USA, protestors tried to get the senate to ban IVF treatment altogether.

Medical fears

Even medical experts were worried. They feared that without more knowledge and tighter legal controls, IVF could cause serious problems. Babies might be born with disabilities if eggs, sperm or embryos were accidentally damaged in the laboratory. And women undergoing IVF might agree to new, more dangerous procedures, and risk their lives in their desperate desire to have a child. Experts warned that without ethical guidelines and tighter legal controls, IVF could cause serious problems.

The movie Terminator (1984) envisaged a future in which humans had lost control of their own technology, which had unleashed terror in the form of a part-human, part-machine 'cyborg'.

Today, in the early years of the 21st century, IVF techniques have been greatly developed and improved. Doctors can manage women's hormones in a precise, controlled way, and also improve the fertilizing power of men's sperm. In many countries, IVF is no longer surprising or controversial, but simply a matter of routine. No-one knows the precise figure, but experts estimate that over half a million IVF babies have been born worldwide.

ZIFT and GIFT

Doctors have also used the knowledge learned from early IVF procedures to develop other new techniques for treating infertility. These include ZIFT – a process where an egg fertilized in a glass dish is replaced almost immediately in a woman's Fallopian tube, rather than her uterus. Doctors think this allows it to develop more naturally. A similar technique, called GIFT, places a carefully chosen egg and some selected sperm separately in a woman's Fallopian tube so that fertilization can take place there. Both these techniques involve quite major surgery for the woman. They can work well, but it has not yet been proved whether they are any more successful than IVF.

A group of IVF children and their parents enjoy a get-together at 'The Angel of the North' sculpture in the north of England .

AN EVERYDAY *operation*

IVF treatment is now an everyday operation – at least, in wealthy countries. In 1998, 20 years after Louise Brown was born, an American radio journalist reported: *'More than 350 American clinics perform the procedure some 40,000 times annually. An estimated 45,000 American offspring have been conceived by IVF since 1981'*.

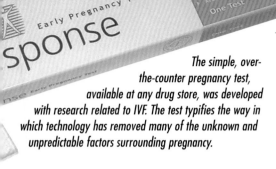

The simple, over-the-counter pregnancy test, available at any drug store, was developed with research related to IVF. The test typifies the way in which technology has removed many of the unknown and unpredictable factors surrounding pregnancy.

ICSI
In the 1990s, doctors invented another new infertility treatment, using amazingly delicate techniques to handle eggs and sperm. Known as ICSI (Intracytoplasmic Sperm Injection), this process involves isolating just one sperm, picking it up with an ultra-fine needle, and injecting it into a woman's egg so that the two may fuse and fertilize. Many doctors hope that ICSI will turn out to be more successful than IVF, especially in cases where there are problems with a man's sperm.

Sharing fertility
New information about fertility, learned from IVF, has also been used to help couples who cannot have children even through using this process. If their eggs or sperm are damaged, the woman can be given healthy ones taken from donors. In some countries, such as the USA, infertile women can become pregnant by being given another couple's embryos, fertilized in the laboratory from donors' eggs and sperm.

Wider uses
Close monitoring techniques such as ultrasound, developed to check the progress of IVF treatment, have also helped save the lives of many pregnant women and their unborn babies. And the intensive study of women's hormones has also helped invent new treatments for several serious female diseases, such as breast cancer.

Since 1978, IVF has brought great joy to many families. Now that the first IVF babies have grown into healthy adults, it seems clear that many of the early fears about 'monster children' or 'Frankenstein families' were groundless. But IVF still has many critics. Why?

High cost
IVF is very expensive. On average, each attempt to conceive costs between £2,000–£3,000. In the UK and other countries with national health services, IVF treatment is not always provided by the state. In countries where families rely on private health-insurance schemes, these do not usually pay for IVF. As a result, poor couples cannot afford fertility treatments, and the chance of having children through this amazing treatment becomes a privilege available only to the rich.

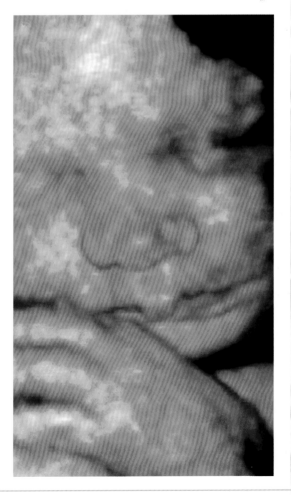

'….it is only since the breakthrough with IVF that so many couples who would have remained childless have been able to experience the natural joy of parenthood. My twins, a girl and a boy, were born healthy in February 1998, the family I always dreamed of, they just took a bit longer than I anticipated. Ask me… what the birth of Louise Brown meant to me and I will tell you, it changed my life.'

A British woman who became a mother after successful IVF treatment.

Ultrasound is a process that was developed to monitor IVF. A probe is passed over the woman's abdomen and transmits an image of the foetus on to a screen.

WORTH *every penny?*

In 1999, Britain's BBC news reported how one couple had spent about £35,000 on 11 IVF treatments before finally giving birth to twins.

Unfair Because of these high costs, many people feel uneasy about spending so much money to treat infertile women when millions of mothers in poor countries suffer during pregnancy and die in childbirth from easily-treatable conditions. And they also worry whether it is right to help produce babies by expensive IVF when many young children in poor or war-torn lands are homeless, hungry, orphaned, or suffering from killer diseases. They argue that the money used for IVF would be better spent on care for these vulnerable people.

Dangerous Critics also say that IVF can be very dangerous for women. In the 1970s and 1980s, with the best of intentions, doctors often placed several embryos inside a patient's uterus after test-tube fertilization. They hoped this would increase the chances of conception. Doctors in private fertility clinics, which are mostly run as businesses, did the same because they were under great pressure to succeed. This led to some women becoming pregnant with three or more foetuses at a time. This was dangerous for them, and also for their unborn babies. The foetuses often died in the uterus, or were born too early to survive. Alternatively, the would-be parents would have to make the difficult decision to ask doctors to

With so many children, such as this one in Ethiopia, suffering from famine and disease, critics of IVF ask whether it is right to produce babies through such an expensive treatment.

kill some of the foetuses inside the woman's body, so that the others had a chance to live.

Disabilities
If babies from these 'multiple pregnancies' did manage to survive, they often had serious mental or physical disabilities. Today, many countries limit the number of embryos that can be placed in the uterus to three, and some doctors prefer to only use one or two. Recently, critics of new infertility techniques such as ICSI fear that these methods could lead to many babies being born with genetic diseases.

Ethics
As well as causing medical controversy, IVF and other fertility treatments raise big issues about how we use scientific and medical discoveries, and even about human rights. People are asking questions about the purpose of love, sex and marriage, and about the rights and duties of parents. Fertility treatments have even been seen by some as a threat to civilization itself.

Painful failure
From its beginnings, IVF has been criticized for putting couples under tremendous strain. It can raise unrealistic hopes that end in cruel disappointment. It can be painful, physically and emotionally. Only 22% of all IVF treatments succeed, which means that most couples who try it experience failure, often several times. This failure can lead to depression, and put a heavy strain on relationships.

British journalist Liz Tilberis (shown on right of picture to the left), a former editor of Vogue magazine, believed that fertility treatment was the cause of her ovarian cancer. She criticized people's reluctance to accept that the treatment is potentially harmful for many women.

WORTH *dying for?*

A few people even think that the hormone procedure used to stimulate a woman's ovaries during IVF treatment can trigger very serious diseases of her reproductive organs. For example, British journalist Liz Tilberis believed that the nine IVF treatments she had before giving birth to her sons led to her developing cancer of the ovaries, from which she died in 1999. Doctors say they can find no evidence to support her views, but research continues.

Many women and men feel 'incomplete' if they do not manage to have a child of their own. Many feel they must try IVF, as a 'last chance', because it is an option. The fact that they have invested a great deal of time and money in it often makes them feel much worse if they are unsuccessful.

The right to a child?

Some people argue that IVF helps couples achieve their 'right' to have a child. Others say that there is no such right, but that instead, men and women should learn to accept their childlessness with dignity. Many are horrified when women long past their natural child-bearing years become pregnant with IVF, as in the case of one Italian woman aged 62. But this birth was in fact welcomed by test-tube pioneer Dr Robert Edwards, who commented, '…the (older) ladies themselves don't think it is bad and I think (they) … are to be supported'.

This teenager suffers from cystic fibrosis, a hereditary disease that can cause respiratory infections. Scientists think that his condition could one day be cured using the controversial research being carried out with embryos.

ACCEPTING *fate*

Improved medical knowledge learned through IVF can help doctors understand why some couples are infertile. But it cannot always help infertile men and women cope with the sense of unfairness that many of them feel. They often ask, 'why me?' In 1998, Professor Ian Craft, London fertility treatment expert, commented: *'Before IVF, people accepted their lot, because they couldn't do anything about it. Now they question it'*.

The right to life? IVF and other fertility treatments have also been criticized by 'right to life' campaigners. They argue that life begins at conception, and that embryos created but not used during IVF treatments are 'murdered' when doctors use them for scientific experiments, or dispose of them. Their opponents claim that life starts at a much later date – when a foetus has grown enough to survive outside the uterus – and that information gained by studying 'spare' embryos may help cure many diseases.

Legal limits States can make laws to control IVF procedures. In Britain, for example, a watchdog body called the HFEA (Human Fertilisation and Embryology Authority) was set up in 1991. But human feelings are often much more complicated than a lawyer's rules, and IVF techniques remain controversial. This is especially so when mistakes are made, such as in 2002 when eggs and sperm got muddled up at a British hospital and a woman gave birth to babies fathered by the wrong man. This raised perplexing questions, especially for the child. Their biological parent was known, but who should care for them, and give them love? Who should be their legal guardian? And who should they call 'Daddy?'

Pressure groups, such as those opposed to abortion, sometimes lobby governments and take direct action. These groups feel that moral attitudes – to the family, and to the sanctity of life itself – are being threatened by science such as embryo research.

ouise Brown, the world's first test-tube baby, is now a fit, healthy adult. She owes her life to the IVF technique but, perhaps surprisingly, she is reported as saying that she would not want IVF treatment for herself. More than a million people, however, – parents, scientists and family friends – would not agree with her. Since 1978, IVF has brought joy and great satisfaction to many lives.

By waiting to produce an embryo with the right tissue, British couple Mr and Mrs Hashimi hope to save their son Zain's life. This is one of the most obvious situations where couples would benefit from having the right to choose a certain type of embryo.

Helping nature
IVF was shocking at first, but it is now widely accepted. We now know that the technique is usually safe for mothers, and that children conceived by IVF are generally healthy. In some ways, IVF is not so revolutionary after all – it is simply helping nature. The only difference between IVF and natural conception is the place – a glass dish – where egg and sperm join together and fertilize. Once the embryo is returned to the mother's uterus, then pregnancy continues naturally.

Life-saving
IVF treatments have also made many other techniques possible. Some have the power to save lives. In 2002, British parents Raj and Shahana Hashmi sought legal permission to screen their embryos before going ahead with a pregnancy. They are looking for a suitable tissue match in the embryo for their sick son Zain, who has a dangerous blood disorder called thalassaemia. The hope is that if a matching embryo is allowed to be born, the blood in its umbilical cord be used to treat Zain.

Genetic engineering
Many people feel alarmed at the possibility of changing the genetic code within embryos to create 'designer

FUTURE choices

Many people are excited and concerned in equal measure at the breakthroughs now being achieved in the field of genetic research. The Church of England has reacted with unease to statements such as that by Dean Hamer, of the American National Cancer Institute, when he declared in 1995: _'We will soon have the power to change and manipulate human behaviour through genetics.'_ John Habgood, the Archbishop of York, summed up the views of many thinkers with this comment: _'[We must be] suspicious about improving human nature, and even more suspicious of those who think they know what improvements ought to be made.'_

A DANGEROUS *race*

• In 2002, rival scientists Severino Antinori from Italy, and Panayiotis Zavos from the USA both claimed to be close to producing cloned humans.

• On December 26th, 2002, members of the Raelian Movement claimed to have produced the world's first cloned human – 'Baby Eve' – although no independent scientist has confirmed the birth, or seen the baby.

• In February 2003, Dolly the sheep, the world's first cloned mammal, was put to sleep. She was six years old. She had aged much more quickly than normal sheep, and was in pain from severe arthritis – a disease of old age.

babies'. It may soon be possible to engineer an embryo's character, as well as physical characteristics like hair colour. This raises many ethical and moral questions: what kinds of behaviour should be bred in future humans? What kind of behaviour should be removed? And who, if anyone, should have the power to choose? Genetic engineering is, however, currently banned in many countries.

Cloning IVF treatment

also helped to develop one of the most controversial scientific achievements of the late 20th century – cloning. A clone is a copy of just one parent, and is not produced by normal fertilization. The technique is not easy, and is still far from perfect. It took scientists in Scotland 277 attempts to produce the world's first cloned mammal, Dolly the sheep. Most cloned animals born so far have had genetic defects. Cloning is also banned in many parts of the world.

No easy answers In 2002,

test-tube pioneer Dr Edwards said he would back human cloning – but only if the process was proven to be safe. Other fertility experts disagreed. As with all important questions, there are no easy answers. We must think carefully about what we want for ourselves, and what kind of society we want to live in, before we make this difficult decision.

Are we on the threshold of a future in which it may be possible to 'choose' babies for their athletic potential, their mental abilities or their appearance?

1500–1784

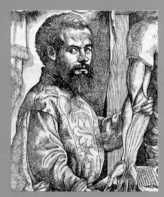

- **1537:** Flemish doctor Andreas Vesalius establishes the modern science of anatomy with his book *Six Anatomical Pictures*. It is the first to contain accurate drawings of human bones and organs. Vesalius makes his discoveries using corpses of executed criminals.

- **1561:** Italian anatomist Gabriele Falloppia accurately describes the woman's Fallopian tubes in his book *Anatomical Observations*. Doctors then realize that infertility could be caused by damaged Fallopian tubes.

- **1677:** Dutch scientist Anton van Leeuwenhoek, a pioneer microscopist, is the first to see sperm under a microscope — calling them 'human larvae'. He believes that babies are formed from sperm alone.

- **1777:** An Italian priest experiments with the artificial insemination of reptiles.

1785–1890

- **1785:** British scientist John Hunter unsuccessfully attempts artificial insemination.

- **1828–1837:** Estonian naturalist Karl Ernst von Baer pioneers the study of embryology. His book, *Developmental History of Animals*, is the first to explain how ovaries work in humans and animals.

- **1843:** British doctor Martin Barry discovers how a human sperm and egg fuse together at the moment of fertilization. It becomes clear that both male and female cells play an equally important part in conception.

- **1868:** German scientist Adolf Kussmaul invents the gastroscope (a pipe fitted with lamp and lenses) for examining inside the stomach. Its invention gives rise to the laparoscope, which enables scientists to examine the sex organs in much greater detail.

- **1890:** British scientist Robert Dickinson conducts experiments with donor sperm. He has to continue his work in secret after condemnation by the Catholic church.

1891–1948

- **1929–1930:** American scientists Edgar Allen and Edward Doisy identify the main female sex hormone, called 'oestrogen'.

- **1934:** German biochemist Adolf Butenandt discovers the second main female sex hormone called progesterone, which prepares the Fallopian tube and uterus to receive an egg.

- **1948:** A report on artificial insemination published in the *British Medical Journal* sparks a fierce debate in parliament. The Church of England recommends that the practice be made a criminal offence. The British government declares the practice 'undesirable and not to be encouraged'.

1949–1966

- **1953:** British biologist Francis Crick and American biologist James Watson construct a molecular model of DNA. This opens the way to research into the genetic makeup of all living things.

- **1965:** British biologist Robert Edwards experiments with techniques for keeping unripe eggs alive in a culture medium (mixture of chemicals).

- **1966:** Robert Edwards teams up with British gynaecologist Patrick Steptoe. They use a laparoscope to remove ripe eggs from ovaries and fertilise them with sperm outside the woman's body.

1967–1977

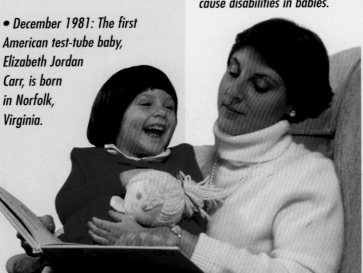

- 1972: Edwards and Steptoe place eggs fertilized in the laboratory back inside the bodies of women with damaged Fallopian tubes, hoping that the eggs will implant in the uterus. They make more than 80 unsuccessful attempts.

- 1975: British woman Marlene Platt is the first to conceive by the new infertility treatment known as IVF. However, the pregnancy is ectopic and has to be terminated.

- November, 1977: British couple Lesley and John Brown begin IVF treatment after hearing of the work of Edwards and Steptoe. Lesley Brown conceives after an egg fertilized with her husband's sperm is placed in her uterus.

1978–1989

- July 1978: Following a Caesarian operation, Lesley Brown gives birth to the first test-tube baby, named Louise Joy.

- December 1981: The first American test-tube baby, Elizabeth Jordan Carr, is born in Norfolk, Virginia.

- 1988: The first pregnancies are achieved as a result of GIFT — a technique whereby egg and sperm are placed separately inside the uterus and are allowed to fertilize there.

1990–1992

- 1990: The Human Fertilisation and Embryology Act is passed in the UK.

- 1991: Also established is a watchdog body, the Human Fertilisation and Embryology Authority (HFEA), which aims to control IVF procedures.

- January, 1992: The first successful pregnancy is announced as a result of a new treatment known as ICSI (Intracytoplasmic Sperm Injection). Critics warn it may cause disabilities in babies.

- May, 1992: A 62-year-old Italian woman named Rosanna della Corta gives birth to a son, Riccardo, after IVF treatment by Dr Severino Antinori.

1993–2002

- 1996: A Scottish sheep, named Dolly, is the first mammal to be successfully cloned after 277 unsuccessful attempts.

- 2000: A culture using embryonic stem cells, some from 'spare' embryos donated by couples who have received IVF, opens the way to 'made-to-order' tissue for transplant surgery.

- 2002: British couple Raj and Shahana Hashimi seek right to screen embryos before going ahead with pregnancy, hoping to have a baby with the right tissue to provide cord blood to save the life of their son.

- August, 2002: Rival scientists Severino Antinori from Italy, and Panayiotis Zavos from the USA both claim to be close to producing cloned humans.

- December, 2002: An organization called the Raelian Movement claims to have produced the world's first cloned human — 'baby Eve'. However, no independent scientist has confirmed the legitamcy of the claim, or seen the baby.

amniocentesis The sampling of fluid taken from the womb during the course of pregnancy. This is done to assess the condition of a foetus.

anatomy The branch of biology or medicine that deals with the structure of bodies or plants. Knowledge of conception, pregnancy and infertility increased rapidly after Andreas Vesalius (1514–64) first published accurate drawings of humans bones and organs.

artificial insemination The fertilization of an egg with sperm by methods other than through sexual intercourse.

Caesarian section An operation to deliver a baby by cutting open the abdomen and removing the baby directly from the uterus.

cloning The copying of cells or organisms 'asexually' — from one parent, without normal fertilization. The development of this controversial practice was aided by the discoveries stemming from IVF.

DNA Deoxyribonucleic acid. The genetic material contained within the cells of all living things. It governs cell growth and is responsible for passing genetic information from one generation to the next.

ectopic pregnancy A pregnancy where the fertilized egg implants and starts to grow outside the uterus. Ectopic pregnancies are terminated because the growing baby can cause internal bleeding that may endanger the mother.

embryo The name given to an unborn offspring during the first eight weeks after conception. Once an egg has been fertilized by sperm, and has started to grow, it becomes an embryo.

foetus The name given to an unborn, developing offspring of more than eight weeks after conception. Some argue that an embryo becomes a foetus at an even earlier stage.

fertilization The joining of a single sperm with a ripe egg, either inside the Fallopian tubes or outside the woman's body if she is undergoing IVF treatment.

egg The female reproductive cell, also called an ovum. Eggs are produced in the woman's ovaries. Every 28 days or so, a ripe egg is released from a bubble on the ovary called a follicle. The egg is then collected by the funnel-shaped opening of the Fallopian tube, and carried along the Fallopian tube, where it will survive for only one or two days unless fertilized by sperm.

Fallopian tubes Ducts through which eggs travel to the uterus once released from the ovaries. Eggs are fertilized by sperm that have swum into the Fallopian tubes.

genetic engineering The artificial manipulation of genes contained within the cells of living things. This may allow parents to select only those embryos without defects or embryos with particular characteristics. Research into cells taken from embryos may enable doctors to produce 'made-to-order' tissue for transplant surgery. The matter is highly controversial.

GIFT Gamete Intrafallopian transfer. A technique where an egg and some sperm are placed separately in a Fallopian tube, so that fertilization can take place there.

gynaecology The branch of medicine that deals with diseases and disorders of women, especially of the female reproductive system. A gynaecologist is a doctor who specialises in this field.

HFEA The Human Fertilisation and Embryology Authority. A watchdog body set up in the UK in 1990 to regulate and control IVF practices.

hormone A chemical released directly into the bloodstream by a gland or tissue and which plays important roles in fertilization, conception and pregnancy. The two main female hormones are 'oestrogen', which causes women to become sexually mature and 'progesterone', which prepares the Fallopian tubes and uterus to receive a fertilized egg. In some IVF treatments, hormones are given to a woman in order to stimulate her ovaries into producing several ripened eggs.

ICSI Intracytoplasmic Sperm Injection. An infertility treatment developed after IVF. It involves isolating one sperm, picking it up with an ultra-fine needle, and injecting it into an woman's egg so that the two may fuse and fertilize. This treatment may help couples where the infertility problem lies with the man's sperm.

implantation Also called 'nidation'. The point at which a fertilized egg attaches to the lining of the uterus. Conception is complete after implantation has taken place.

infertility The inability to conceive and produce a baby. Doctors consider a woman infertile if she is under 35 and has failed to conceive after a year of unprotected sexual intercourse, or after six months if she is over 35. There are numerous causes of infertility, including blocked or damaged Fallopian tubes, low sperm count and environmental factors such as stress or alcohol abuse.

in vitro fertilization An infertility treatment that involves removing a ripe egg from a woman's body and then mixing it with sperm in a shallow glass dish. The fertilized egg is then returned to the woman's uterus. The name 'in vitro' is Latin for 'in glass'.

laparoscope A fibre-optic tube inserted through the abdominal wall, allowing doctors to observe the body's organs. A laparoscope is used when removing ripe eggs from the uterus of a woman undergoing IVF treatment.

ovaries The pair of female reproductive organs that produce eggs and female sex hormones. The ovaries take turns to produce one egg each month. During IVF treatment, a ripe egg is removed directly from an ovary.

ovulation The process in which a woman produces an egg. About 12 times each year, a ripened egg is released from her ovaries some 14 days before her period. It stays for about 12 hours in the nearest Fallopian tube, where it dies unless fertilized by sperm.

rhesus factor Any of several chemical substances present in red blood cells that can provoke allergic reactions in a woman. If a woman is rhesus negative and her husband is rhesus positive, she may have rhesus compatibility problems. After the first pregnancy, the rhesus factor enters the mother's circulatory system during the birth of a child who has inherited rhesus factor from their father. The mother's body then produces antibodies against it. If she becomes pregnant with another rhesus-positive baby, the antibodies may attack the baby's red blood cells, causing mild to serious anaemia in the baby.

sperm The male sex cells. Sperm are made in two glands called testes. During sexual intercourse, sperm is released from the testes in liquid called semen. Each sperm has a flagellum (tail) that enables it to swim towards the egg in the woman's uterus.

test-tube baby Popular name given to babies born by mothers who have received IVF treatment.

ultrasound A sound of ultra-sonic frequency, which is used by doctors to assess the progress of a pregnancy. A probe transmitting pulses is passed over the woman's abdomen. The pulses reflect back and appear as bright spots on a dark screen, forming an accurate image of the foetus.

uterus The muscular female reproductive organ that houses and nourishes the foetus during pregnancy (also called the 'womb').

ZIFT Zygote Intrafallopian Transfer. An infertility treatment where an egg fertilized in a glass dish is replaced almost immediately in the woman's Fallopian tube, instead of in her uterus. Doctors think this allows the egg to develop more naturally.

A

abortions 39
Abse, Leo 32
adoption 13, 14, 15
Abu ('father of') 8
Allen, Edgar 19, 42
amniocentesis 26, 44
anaesthetic 24, 28
Anatomical Observations 16, 42
anatomy 16, 18, 42, 44
Angel of the North 34
antibodies 13, 45
Antinori, Dr Severino 41, 43
arthritis 41
Associated Press 30

B

Baer, Karl Ernst von 18, 42
Bangalore 30
Barry, Martin 18, 42
BBC (British Broadcasting Corporation) 36
Beecher, Henry Ward 7
belly button 11
birth control 15
blood 10, 12, 13, 17, 26, 45
blood pressure 28
blood type 12
Boleyn, Anne 12
bone marrow 40, 43
bones 26, 42, 44
brains 26, 27
Brave New World 32
breast cancer 35
Bristol 22
Brown, John 22, 23, 28, 30, 43

Brown, Lesley 22, 23, 24, 25, 28, 29, 30, 43
Brown, Louise 4, 5, 6, 29, 30, 32, 34, 35, 40, 43
Brown, Natalie 30
Brown-Séquard, Charles 21
Butenandt, Adolf 19, 42

C

Caesarian sections 28, 43, 44
cancer 37
Carr, Elizabeth Jordan 31, 43
cell division 10
cells 10, 18, 20, 21, 25, 43, 44
chromosomes 10
cloning 6, 7, 41, 43, 44
conception 9, 11, 17, 18, 39, 40, 42, 44, 45
contraceptive pill 6
Cornelia 8
corpses 16, 42
Corta, Rosanna della 43
Craft, Professor Ian 39
Crick, Francis 20, 42
culture medium 21, 24, 42
cyborgs 33
cystic fibrosis 38

D

designer babies 41
Developmental History of Animals 18, 42
Dickinson, Robert 42
diseases 7, 16, 35, 36, 37
dissections 16
divorce 32
DNA (Deoxyribonucleic Acid)

20, 42, 44
doctors 5, 11, 16, 17, 20, 24, 29, 30, 31, 34, 36, 37, 38, 39, 42, 44, 45
dogs 18
Doisy, Edward 19, 42
Dolly the sheep 41, 43
Donald, Ian 20

E

Edwards, Dr Robert 5, 21, 22, 24, 25, 28, 30, 31, 33, 38, 41, 42, 43
eggs (ova) 5, 9, 10, 11, 12, 13, 16, 17, 18, 19, 20, 21, 22, 23, 24, 25, 31, 33, 34, 35, 39, 40, 42, 43, 44, 45
Egypt, ancient 9
electron microscopes 5
embryos 17, 25, 26, 28, 31, 33, 35, 36, 37, 38, 39, 40, 41, 43, 44
endoscopes 18
Ethiopia 36
Europe 14
Eve 9, 41, 43
eyes 17, 27

F

Fallopian tubes 10, 17, 19, 20, 21, 22, 24, 34, 42, 43, 44, 45
Falloppia, Gabriele 16, 17, 42
family planning 32
fertility charm 4, 13
fertilization 6, 9, 10, 11, 20, 23, 24, 25, 34, 36, 40, 41,

42, 43, 44, 45
foetuses 17, 28, 36, 37, 38, 44, 45
fostering 12, 14, 15
foster parents 14
foundlings 12
Frankenstein 32

G

gastroscopes 18, 42
genes 9, 44
    'selfish genes' 9
gene therapy 6
genetic defects 41
genetic engineering 31, 40, 44
gibbets 16
GIFT (Gamete Intrafallopian Transfer) 34, 43, 44
Good Housekeeping 30
gynaecologists 21, 44

H

Hashimi, Raj and Shahana 40, 43
HCG 26
heart transplants 22
Henry VIII 12
HFEA (Human Fertilisation and Embryology Authority) 39, 43, 44
homosexuality 32
hormones 19, 21, 24, 26, 34, 35, 37, 42, 44, 45
human rights 37
Hunter, John 42
Huxley, Aldous 32

I

ICSI (Intracytoplasmic Sperm Injection) 35, 37, 43, 45
immune systems 13
incubators 22, 24
India 30
infertility 4, 5, 6, 11, 12, 17, 18, 19, 20, 22, 23, 30, 37, 43, 44, 45
IVF (In Vitro Fertilisation) 4, 5, 6, 22, 23, 26, 28, 29, 30, 31, 32, 33, 34, 35, 36, 37, 38, 39, 40, 41, 43, 44, 45

J

Jones, Dr Howard 31

K

Kalyan, Dr Brij 30
Kussmaul, Adolf 18, 42

L

laboratories 5, 6, 21, 32, 33, 43
labour 17
laparoscopes 18, 21, 24, 42, 45
Leeuwenhoek, Anton van 17, 42
Lind, Jenny 9
lungs 26, 27

M

magic amulets 12
menstrual cycle 24
mice 19
midwives 17

N

nidation (implantation) 10, 45
Nobel Prizes 19, 20

O

Oldham 22
Oldham General Hospital 4
oestrogen 19, 42, 45
On How the Body is Made 16
organ transplants 6
orphans 13
ovaries 10, 17, 19, 20, 21, 24, 37, 42, 44, 45
ovulation 11, 45

P

Padua, university of 16
pigs 19, 31
pilgrimages 12
pill, contraceptive 15
Platt, Marlene 21, 43
prayers 12
pre-eclampsia 28
pregnancies 9, 15, 19, 21, 25, 28, 32, 35, 36, 37, 38, 40, 43, 44, 45
   ectopic 20, 21, 43, 44
pregnancy tests 35
progesterone 19, 42, 45
psychologists 33
puberty 10

Q

quads 5
quintets 5

R

Rael 7
Raelian Cult 7, 41, 43
Ramses II 9
Renaissance 16
reproduction 8, 10
reproductive organs 16, 18, 37, 44
Renoir, Pierre Auguste 8
rhesus factor 13, 45
   rhesus negative 12, 13
Roman Catholics 12, 32, 42

S

SEM (Scanning Electron Microscope) 18
septuplets 6
sex organs 10
Shelley, Mary 32
Six Anatomical Pictures 16, 42
skeletons 16, 26
social workers 14
sperm 5, 6, 9, 10, 11, 13, 17, 18, 20, 21, 23, 24, 25, 31, 33, 34, 35, 39, 40, 42, 43, 44, 45
state benefits 8
stem cells 43
Steptoe, Dr Patrick 5, 21, 22, 23, 24, 25, 28, 30, 31, 33, 38, 42, 43
stomachs 18, 42

T

Terminator 33
testes 10, 19
Tilberis, Liz 37
toxaemia 28
triplets 5
tubal disease 19
twins 5

U

ultrasound 20, 26, 35, 45
umbilical cord 11
Umm ('mother of') 8
USA 14
uterine cavities 17
uterine linings 17, 19, 25

V

vaginas 10, 17, 25
Vesalius, Andreas 16, 42, 44
virgins 15
Vogue magazine 37

W

Watson, James 20, 42
wombs (uteri) 7, 9, 10, 17, 19, 20, 25, 26, 28, 34, 36, 37, 39, 40, 43, 44, 45

X

x-rays 21

Z

Zavos, Panayiotis 41, 43
ZIFT (Zygote Intrafallopian Transfer) 34

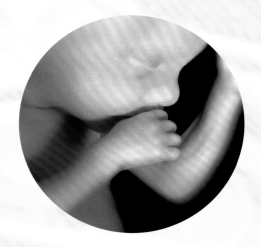

Copyright © ticktock Entertainment Ltd 2003
First published in Great Britain in 2003 by ticktock Media Ltd.,
Unit 2, Orchard Business Centre, North Farm Road, Tunbridge Wells, Kent, TN2 3XF

ISBN 1 86007 420 0 pbk
ISBN 1 86007 427 8 hbk
Printed in Taiwan

A CIP catalogue record for this book is available from the British Library.

We would like to thank: Tall Tree Ltd, Lizzy Bacon and Ed Simkins for their assistance.

10 9 8 7 6 5 4 3 2 1

Picture Credits
Every effort has been made to trace the copyright holders, and we apologize in advance for any unintentional omissions.
We would be pleased to insert the appropriate acknowledgements in any subsequent edition of this publication.

B = bottom; C = centre; L = left; R = right; T = top.
Alamy: 12–13c, 35b, 43c. Corbis: 8–9, 10–11, 12, 18b, 20t, 39, 42b. Hulton Archive: 28b. NASA: 1, 6–7c, 7t, 15b, 19t, 22t, 30–31, 32–33,
34, 35t, 36–37, 38, 40, 43c, 43r. Science Photo Library: 6, 14l, 22t, 25, 26–27.

10.99